THE MUMBAI ATTACK COLOUR

26/11

MR VIVEK KUMAR PANDEY SHAMBHUNATH

ISBN 979-888546527-4

During writing this book no character & no religious are harmed written by Mr Vivek Kumar Pandey. Winner Youngest Writer Award 1st Rank In India 2020.He Is Only One Writer Can Publish 700+ Own Book That Was Greatest Successfull In His Life.In This Book Deeply Given About Mumbai terrorist attacks of 2008, multiple terrorist attacks that occurred on November 26–29, 2008, in Mumbai (Bombay), Maharashtra, India.This book fully colour edition books.

Contents

Foreword

Author biography in English :MY NAME IS VIVEK KUMAR PANDEY . I WAS BORN IN 30 SEP 2002,I AM FROM SURAT GUJARAT INDIA.MY DREAM WAS TO BE GOOD WRITERS ,MY FAMILY SUPPORTED ME TO SUCCESSFUL AND I CAN DO IT MY SELF.How do I write? That is a question, I believe, that can be honestly answered by me."CELEBRATING YOUNGEST WRITER AWARD WINNER IN GUJARAT 1ST RANK" MR PANDEY JI . I may think I did a good job writing something when in reality it could be horrible. The reader is the one who decides the quality of my writing. I do find writing to be natural to me and therefore find it to be a real challenge. My trick as a challenged writer is to do the best I can and know that I am happy with the final outcome. It may take a while to do my best and there may be quite a few problems I run into along the way.

I am not a greedy person those who are thinking about me and my self I never tried it anyone people suffering from sadness ,I trying to get promoted people suffering from happiness and joy in your Life Time. Now in current situation in India and also world people are unemployed and have no many but our indian governor help to people to get free food from ration card , i also take part in leadership team ,i am Motivational speaker , Film script writer. There was my two dream firstly writer and secondly actor & also my own film is upcoming soon i done almost completely completed script for my film .I AM GOING TO SAY WORD OF HEART TOUCH OUT PLEASE READ IT" , firstly i thanks my father he supports me in this field they always getting inspired me by own his words and behavior ,they always said that he was a biggest person in the world in future and also they purchase fruit and chocolate for me in anytime & anyway , firstly my father buy him then call me Vivek you want a chocolate i will say yes papa but how many tell me ,papa: you tell me how much i buy him i told 1 or 2 chocolate but my father purchase whole the boxes of chocolate and they get suprised me. MY FATHER WAS BORN IN " 20 SEPTEMBER" 1971 IN INDIA.

1) MY FATHER FAVORITE CLOTHES IS KURTA PAIJMA AND ALSO STYLES SHOE

2) FAVORITE SINGER IS KISHORE DA

3) FAVORITE STATE GUJARAT AND KOLKATA , HIS VILLAGE IN BIHAR

4) FAVORITE COLOR BLACK AND WHITE

THEY ALSO LOVE cricket like IPL and one day t-20 .they also like watching a News daily and heard the song daily ,they also interested in tik tok video but in current time tik tok is banned in india but also few videos are in you tube. In lockdown time my family and me very enjoy day daily. my father play daily ludo with his sister and son, daughter.they always loved tea and coffee anytime call me "। विवेक थोड़ा चाय बनाओना विवेक तुम्हारे हाथ का चाय अच्छा लगता है". I make it tea for my father but some reason after the April to june they are suffering from fever and cough , weakness on 6 June 2020 my father death. they not told me say bye bye his life. After death of 6 June on 10 june my mom and dad anniversary.but my father is Best in the world they can do anything for me please take care of father and respect it of your parents.

CHAPTER ONE

2008 Mumbai attacks

- 2008 Mumbai attacks

The 2008 Mumbai attacks as 26/11 were a series of terrorist attacks that took place in November 2008, when 10 members of Lashkar-e-Taiba, an Islamist terrorist organisation from Pakistan, carried out 12 coordinated shooting and bombing attacks lasting four days across Mumbai. The attacks, which drew widespread global condemnation, began on Wednesday 26 November and lasted until Saturday 29 November 2008. A total of 175 people died, including nine attackers, and more than 300 were wounded.

- Eight of the attacks occurred in South Mumbai: at Chhatrapati Shivaji Terminus, the Oberoi Trident, the Taj Palace & Tower,the Leopold Cafe, the Cama Hospital, the Nariman House, the Metro Cinema, and in a lane behind the Times of India building and St. Xavier's College.There was also an explosion at Mazagaon, in Mumbai's port area, and in a taxi at Vile Parle. By the early morning of 28 November, all sites except for the Taj Hotel had been secured by the Mumbai Police and security forces. On 29 November, India's National Security Guards (NSG) conducted Operation Black Tornado to flush out the remaining attackers; it culminated in the death of the last remaining attackers at the Taj Hotel and ended the attacks.

Ajmal Kasab, the sole surviving attacker, disclosed that the attackers were members of the terrorist group Lashkar-e-Taiba, among others. The Government of India stated that the attackers came from Pakistan, and their controllers were in Pakistan. Pakistan later confirmed that the sole surviving perpetrator of the attacks was a Pakistani citizen.[On 9 April

2015, the foremost ringleader of the attacks, Zakiur Rehman Lakhvi, was released on bail and disappeared he was arrested again in Lahore on 2 January 2021. In 2018, former Pakistani prime minister Nawaz Sharif suggested that the Pakistani government played a role in the 2008 Mumbai attack.

- Terrorist attacks in Mumbai

There had been many terrorist attacks in Mumbai since the 13 coordinated bomb explosions that killed 257 people and injured 700 on 12 March 1993. The 1993 attacks were carried out in revenge for earlier religious riots that killed many Muslims.

On 6 December 2002, a blast in a BEST bus near Ghatkopar station killed two people and injured 28. The bombing occurred on the 10th anniversary of the demolition of the Babri Mosque in Ayodhya. A bicycle bomb exploded near the Vile Parle station in Mumbai, killing one person and injuring 25 on 27 January 2003, a day before the visit of the Prime Minister of India Atal Bihari Vajpayee to the city. On 13 March 2003, a day after the 10th anniversary of the 1993 Bombay bombings, a bomb exploded in a train compartment near the Mulund station, killing 10 people and injuring 70.

On 28 July 2003, a blast in a BEST bus in Ghatkopar killed 4 people and injured 32. On 25 August 2003, two bombs exploded in South Mumbai, one near the Gateway of India and the other at Zaveri Bazaar in Kalbadevi. At least 44 people were killed and 150 injured. On 11 July 2006, seven bombs exploded within 11 minutes on the Suburban Railway in Mumbai, killing 209 people, including 22 foreigners and more than 700 injured. According to the Mumbai Police, the bombings were carried out by Lashkar-e-Taiba and Students Islamic Movement of India (SIMI).

- Training

A group of men, sometimes stated as 24 and at other times 26,received training in marine warfare at a remote camp in mountainous Muzaffarabad in Pakistan. Part of the training was reported to have taken place on the Mangla Dam reservoir in Pakistan.The recruits went through the following stages of training, according to Indian and US media reports.

Psychological: Indoctrination to Islamist Jihadi ideas, including imagery of atrocities suffered by Muslims in India, Chechnya, Palestine and across the globe.Basic Combat: Lashkar's basic combat training and methodology course, the Daura Aam.Advanced Training: Selected to undergo advanced combat training at a camp near Mansehra, a course the organisation calls the Daura Khaas. According to an unnamed source at the US Defense Department this includes advanced weapons and explosives training supervised by former members of the Pakistan Army, along with survival training and further indoctrination.

Commando Training: Finally, an even smaller group selected for specialized commando tactics training and marine navigation training given to the Fedayeen unit selected in order to target Mumbai.From the recruits, ten were handpicked for the Mumbai mission. They also received training in swimming and sailing, besides the use of high-end weapons and explosives under the supervision of LeT commanders. According to a media report citing an unnamed former Defence Department Official of the US, the intelligence agencies of the US had determined that former officers from Pakistan's Army and Inter-Services Intelligence agency assisted actively and continuously in training.They were given blueprints of all the four targets – The Taj Mahal Palace Hotel, Oberoi Trident, Nariman House and Chhatrapati Shivaji Maharaj Terminus.

- the 2008 Mumbai attacks

The first events were detailed around 20:00 Indian Standard Time (IST) on 26 November, when 10 men in inflatable speedboats came ashore at two locations in Colaba. They reportedly told local Marathi-speaking fishermen who asked them who they were to "mind their own business" before they split up and headed two different ways. The fishermen's subsequent report to the police department received little response and local police failed to act.

- Chhatrapati Shivaji Maharaj Terminus

The Chhatrapati Shivaji Maharaj Terminus (CSMT) was attacked by two gunmen, Ismail Khan and Ajmal Kasab.Kasab was later caught alive by the police and identified by eyewitnesses. The attacks began around 21:30 when the two men entered the passenger hall and opened fireusing AK-47 rifles.The attackers killed 58 people and injured 104 others,their assault ending at about 22:45.Security forces and emergency services arrived shortly afterwards. Announcements by a railway announcer, Vishnu Dattaram Zende, alerted passengers to leave the station and saved many lives. The two gunmen fled the scene and fired at pedestrians and police officers in the streets, killing eight police officers. The attackers passed a police station. Knowing that they were outgunned against the heavily armed terrorists, the police officers at the station, instead of confronting the terrorists, decided to switch off the lights and secure the gates.

The attackers then headed towards Cama Hospital with intent to kill patients, but the hospital staff locked all of the patient wards. A team of the Mumbai Anti-Terrorist Squad led by police chief Hemant Karkare searched the Chhatrapati Shivaji Terminus and then left in pursuit of Kasab and Khan. Kasab and Khan opened fire on the vehicle in a lane next to the hospital, and received return fire in response. Karkare, Vijay Salaskar, Ashok Kamte and one of their officers were killed. The only survivor, Constable Arun Jadhav, was severely wounded. Kasab and Khan seized the police vehicle but later abandoned it and seized a passenger car instead.

They then ran into a police roadblock, which had been set up after Jadhav radioed for help. A gun battle then ensued in which Khan was killed and Kasab was wounded. After a physical struggle, Kasab was arrested. A police officer, Tukaram Omble, was also killed when he tried to disarm Kasab by wrestling his weapon away from him.

- Bullet marks left at Leopold Cafe

The Leopold Cafe, a popular restaurant and bar on Colaba Causeway in South Mumbai, was one of the first sites to be attacked. Two attackers, Shoaib alias Soheb and Nazir alias Abu Umer, opened fire on the cafe on the evening of 26 November between 21:30 and 21:48, killing 10 people (including some foreigners) and injuring many more.

- Bomb blasts in taxis

There were two explosions in taxis caused by timer bombs. The first one occurred at 22:40 at Vile Parle, killing the driver and a passenger. The second explosion took place at Wadi Bunder between 22:20 and 22:25. Three people, including the driver of the taxi were killed, and about 15 others were injured.

- The damaged Oberoi Trident hotel

Two hotels, The Taj Mahal Palace Hotel and the Oberoi Trident, were among the four locations targeted. Six explosions were reported at the Taj Hotel – one in the lobby, two in the elevators, three in the restaurant – and one at the Oberoi Trident.At the Taj, firefighters rescued 200 hostages from windows using ladders during the first night.

CNN initially reported on the morning of 27 November 2008 that the hostage situation at the Taj Hotel had been resolved and quoted the police chief of Maharashtra stating that all hostages were freed however, it was learned later that day that there were still two attackers holding hostages, including foreigners, in the Taj Hotel.

- The first floor of the Taj Hotel was completely gutted

A number of European Parliament Committee on International Trade delegates were staying in the Taj Hotel when it was attacked,but none of them were injured. British Conservative Member of the European Parliament (MEP) Sajjad Karim (who was in the lobby when attackers initially opened fire there) and German Social Democrat MEP Erika Mann were hiding in different parts of the building. Also reported present was Spanish MEP Ignasi Guardans, who was barricaded in a hotel room. Another British Conservative MEP, Syed Kamall, reported that he along with several other MEPs left the hotel and went to a nearby restaurant shortly before the attack. Kamall also reported that Polish MEP Jan Masiel was thought to have been sleeping in his hotel room when the attacks started, but eventually left the hotel safely. Kamall and Guardans reported that a Hungarian MEP's assistant was shot. Also caught up in the shooting were the President of Madrid, Esperanza Aguirre, while checking in at the Oberoi Trident, and Indian MP N. N. Krishnadas of Kerala and Gulam Noon while having dinner at a restaurant in the Taj Hotel.

- Nariman House

Front view of the Nariman House a week after the attacks

Nariman House, a Chabad Lubavitch Jewish centre in Colaba known as the Mumbai Chabad House, was taken over by two attackers and several residents were held hostage. Police evacuated adjacent buildings and exchanged fire with the attackers, wounding one. Local residents were told to stay inside. The attackers threw a grenade into a nearby lane, causing no casualties. NSG commandos arrived from Delhi, and a naval helicopter took an aerial survey. During the first day, 9 hostages were rescued from the first floor. The following day, the house was stormed by NSG commandos fast-roping from helicopters onto the roof, covered by snipers positioned in nearby buildings. After a long battle, one NSG commando, Sergeant Gajender Singh Bisht, and both perpetrators were killed Rabbi Gavriel Holtzberg and his wife Rivka Holtzberg, who was six months pregnant, were murdered with four other hostages inside the house by the attackers.

According to radio transmissions picked up by Indian intelligence, the attackers "would be told by their handlers in Pakistan that the lives of Jews were worth 50 times those of non-Jews". Injuries on some of the bodies indicated that they may have been tortured.NSG Commandos beginning the assault on Nariman House by fast-roping onto the terrace.

- NSG raid

During the attacks, both hotels were surrounded by Rapid Action Force personnel and Marine Commandos (MARCOS) and National Security Guards (NSG) commandos. When reports emerged that attackers were receiving television broadcasts, feeds to the hotels were blocked. Security forces stormed both hotels, and all nine attackers were killed by the morning of 29 November. Major Sandeep Unnikrishnan of the NSG was fatally shot during the rescue of Commando Sunil Yadav, who was hit in the leg by a bullet during the rescue operations at Taj. 32 hostages were killed at the Oberoi Trident.

NSG commandos then took on the Nariman house, and a naval helicopter took an aerial survey. During the first day, 9 hostages were rescued from the first floor. The following day, the house was stormed by NSG commandos fast-roping from helicopters onto the roof, covered by snipers positioned in nearby buildings. NSG Commando Sergeant Gajender Singh Bisht, who was part of the team that fast-roped onto Nariman House, died after a long battle in which both perpetrators were also killed. By the morning of 28 November, the NSG had secured the Jewish outreach centre at Nariman House as well as the Oberoi Trident hotel. They also incorrectly believed that the Taj Palace and Towers had been cleared of attackers, and soldiers were leading hostages and holed-up guests to safety, and removing bodies of those killed in the attacks.

However, later news reports indicated that there were still two or three attackers in the Taj, with explosions heard and gunfire exchanged. Fires were also reported at the ground floor of the Taj with plumes of smoke arising from the first floor. The final operation at the Taj Palace hotel was completed by the NSG commandos at 08:00 on 29 November, killing three attackers and resulting in the conclusion of the attacks. The NSG rescued 250 people from the Oberoi, 300 from the Taj and 60 people (members of 12 different families) from Nariman House. In addition, police seized a boat filled with arms and explosives anchored at Mazgaon dock off Mumbai harbour.

- Ajmal Kasab at Chhatrapati Shivaji Terminus with an AK-47 in his hand

The Mumbai attacks were planned and directed by Lashkar-e-Taiba militants inside Pakistan, and carried out by 10 young armed men trained and sent to Mumbai and directed from inside Pakistan via mobile phones and VoIP.

In July 2009 Pakistani authorities confirmed that LeT plotted and financed the attacks from LeT camps in Karachi and Thatta.In November 2009, Pakistani authorities charged seven men they had arrested earlier, of planning and executing the assault.

Mumbai police department originally identified 37 suspects—including two Pakistani army officers—for their alleged involvement in the plot. All but two of the suspects, many of whom are identified only through aliases, are Pakistani. Two more suspects arrested in the United States in October 2009 for other attacks were also found to have been involved in planning the Mumbai attacks. One of these men, Pakistani American David Headley (born Daood Sayed Gilani), was found to have made several trips to India before the attacks and gathered video and GPS information on behalf of the plotters.

In April 2011, the United States issued arrest warrants for four Pakistani men as suspects in the attack. The men, Sajid Mir, Abu Qahafa, Mazhar Iqbal alias "Major Iqbal", are believed to be members of Lashkar-e-Taiba and helped plan and train the attackers.

- Negotiations with Pakistan

Pakistani Prime Minister Yousaf Raza Gillani and President Asif Ali Zardari condemned the attacks. Pakistan promised to assist in the investigation and President Zardari vowed "strong action against any Pakistani elements found involved in the attack".

Pakistan initially denied that Pakistanis were responsible for the attacks, blaming plotters in Bangladesh and Indian criminals, a claim refuted by India, and saying they needed information from India on other bombings first.Pakistani authorities finally agreed that Ajmal Kasab was a Pakistani on 7 January 2009, and registered a case against three other Pakistani nationals.

- The Indian government supplied evidence to Pakistan and other governments, in the form of interrogations, weapons, and call records of conversations during the attacks. In addition, Indian government officials said that the attacks were so sophisticated that they must have had official backing from Pakistani "agencies", an accusation denied by Pakistan.

Under US and UN pressure, Pakistan arrested a few members of Jamaat ud-Dawa and briefly put its founder under house arrest, but he was found to be free a few days later. A year after the attacks, Mumbai police continued to complain that Pakistani authorities were not co-operating by providing information for their investigation. Meanwhile, journalists in Pakistan said security agencies were preventing them from interviewing people from Kasab's village. The then Home Minister P. Chidambaram said the Pakistani authorities had not shared any information about American suspects Headley and Rana, but that the FBI had been more forthcoming.

An Indian report, summarising intelligence gained from India's interrogation of David Headley, was released in October 2010. It alleged that Pakistan's intelligence agency (ISI) had provided support for the attacks by providing funding for reconnaissance missions in Mumbai.The report included Headley's claim that Lashkar-e-Taiba's chief military commander, Zaki-ur-Rahman Lakhvi, had close ties to the ISI. He alleged that "every big action of LeT is done in close coordination with ISI."In 2018, during an interview with newspaper Dawn, Pakistan's former Prime Minister Nawaz Sharif reportedly indirectly accepted Pakistan's involvement in not preventing the Mumbai attacks.

- Police looking for attackers outside Colaba Investigation

According to investigations, the attackers travelled by sea from Karachi, Pakistan, across the Arabian Sea, hijacked the Indian fishing trawler 'Kuber', killed the crew of four, then forced the captain to sail to Mumbai. After murdering the captain, the attackers entered Mumbai on a rubber dinghy. The captain of 'Kuber', Amar Singh Solanki, had earlier been imprisoned for six months in a Pakistani jail for illegally fishing in Pakistani waters.The attackers stayed and were trained by the Lashkar-e-Taiba in a safehouse at Azizabad in Karachi before boarding a small boat for Mumbai.

David Headley was a member of Lashkar-e-Taiba, and between 2002 and 2009 Headley travelled extensively as part of his work for LeT. Headley received training in small arms and countersurveillance from LeT, built a network of connections for the group, and was chief scout in scoping out targets for Mumbai attack having allegedly been given $25,000 in cash in 2006 by an ISI officer known as Major Iqbal.

The officer also helped him arrange a communications system for the attack, and oversaw a model of the Taj Hotel so that gunmen could know their way inside the target, according to Headley's testimony to Indian authorities. Headley also helped ISI recruit Indian agents to monitor Indian troop levels and movements, according to a US official. At the same time, Headley was also an informant for the US Drug Enforcement Administration, and Headley's wives warned American officials of Headley's involvement with LeT and his plotting attacks, warning specifically that the Taj Hotel may be their target.

US officials believed that the Inter-Services Intelligence (I.S.I.) officers provided support to Lashkar-e-Taiba militants who carried out the attacks. Disclosures made by former American intelligence contractor Edward Snowden in 2013 revealed that the Central Intelligence Agency (CIA) had intercepted communications between the Lashkar boat and the LeT headquarters in Pakistan-administered Kashmir and passed the alert on to RAW on 18 November, eight days before the terrorists actually struck Mumbai. In the hours after the attack, the New York City Police Department sent Brandon del Pozo, an official from their Intelligence Division, to investigate the incident in order to understand what vulnerabilities its methods posed for New York City.

The arrest of Zabiuddin Ansari alias Abu Hamza in June 2012 provided further clarity on how the plot was hatched. According to Abu Hamza, the attacks were previously scheduled for 2006, using Indian youth for the job. However, a huge cache of AK-47's and RDX, which were to be used for the attacks, was recovered from Aurangabad in 2006, thus leading to the dismantling of the original plot. Subsequently, Abu Hamza fled to Pakistan and along with Lashkar commanders, scouted for Pakistani youth to be used for the attacks. In September 2007, 10 people were selected for the mission. In September 2008, these people tried sailing to Mumbai from Karachi, but couldn't complete their mission due to choppy waters. These men made a second attempt in November 2008, and successfully managed to execute the final attacks. David Headley's disclosures, that three Pakistani army officers were associated with the planning and execution of the attack were substantiated by Ansari's revelations during his interrogation.After Ansari's arrest, Pakistan's Foreign Office claimed they had received information that up to 40 Indian nationals were involved in the attacks.

- The attackers planned

The attackers had planned the attack several months ahead of time and knew some areas well enough to vanish and reappear after security forces had left. Several sources have quoted Kasab telling the police that the group received help from Mumbai residents. The attackers used at least three SIM cards purchased on the Indian side of the border with Bangladesh.There were also reports of a SIM card purchased in the US state of New Jersey. Police had also mentioned that Faheem Ansari, an Indian Lashkar operative who had been arrested in February 2008, had scouted the Mumbai targets for the November attacks. Later, the police arrested two Indian suspects, Mikhtar Ahmad, who is from Srinagar in Kashmir, and Tausif Rehman, a resident of Kolkata. They supplied the SIM cards, one in Calcutta, and the other in New Delhi.

The attackers used a satellite phone and cell phones to talk to each other as well as their handlers that were based in Pakistan. In transcripts intercepted by Indian authorities between the attackers and their handlers, the handlers provided the attackers with encouragement, tactical advice, and information gained from media coverage. The attackers used both personal cell phones and those obtained from their victims to communicate with each other and the news media. Although the attackers were encouraged to murder hostages, the attackers were in communication with the news media via cell phones to make demands in return for the release of hostages. This was believed to be done in order to further confuse Indian authorities that they were dealing with primarily a hostage situation.

Type 86 Grenades made by China's state-owned Norinco were used in the attacks.There were also indications that the attackers had been taking steroids. The gunman who survived said that the attackers had used Google Earth to familiarise themselves with the locations of buildings used in the attacks.

There were 10 gunmen, nine of whom were subsequently shot dead and one captured by security forces. Witnesses reported that they seemed to be in their early twenties, wore black T-shirts and jeans, and that they smiled and looked happy as they shot their victims.

It was initially reported that some of the attackers were British citizens but the Indian government later stated that there was no evidence to confirm this.Similarly, early reports of 12 gunmen were also later shown to be incorrect.

On 9 December, the 10 attackers were identified by Mumbai police, along with their home towns in Pakistan: Ajmal Amir from Faridkot, Abu Ismail Dera Ismail Khan from Dera Ismail Khan, Hafiz Arshad and Babr Imran from Multan, Javed from Okara, Shoaib from Sialkot, Nazir Ahmed and Nasir from Faisalabad, Abdul Rahman from Arifwalla, and Fahadullah from Dipalpur Taluka. Dera Ismail Khan is in the North-West Frontier Province; the rest of the towns are in Pakistani Punjab.

On 6 April 2010, the Home Minister of Maharashtra State, which includes Mumbai, informed the Assembly that the bodies of the nine killed Pakistani gunmen from the 2008 attack on Mumbai were buried in a secret location in January 2010. The bodies had been in the mortuary of a Mumbai hospital after Muslim clerics in the city refused to let them be buried on their grounds.

- Attackers

Only one of the 10 attackers, Ajmal Kasab, survived the attack. He was hanged in Yerwada jail in 2012. The other nine attackers killed during the onslaught were Hafiz Arshad alias Abdul Rehman Bada, Abdul Rahman Chhota, Javed alias Abu Ali, Fahadullah alias Abu Fahad, Ismail Khan alias Abu Ismail, Babar Imran alias Abu Akasha, Nasir alias Abu Umar, Nazir alias Abu Umer and Shoaib alias Abu Soheb.

- Arrests Ajmal Kasab and Zabiuddin Ansari

Ajmal Kasab was the only attacker arrested alive by police. At first, he deposed to police inspector Ramesh Mahale that he had come to India "to see Amitabh Bachchan's bungalow", and that he was apprehended by the Mumbai Police outside the bungalow. Much of the information about the attackers' preparation, travel, and movements comes from his subsequent confessions to the Mumbai police.

On 12 February 2009, Pakistan's Interior Minister Rehman Malik said that Pakistani national Javed Iqbal, who acquired VoIP phones in Spain for the Mumbai attackers, and Hamad Ameen Sadiq, who had facilitated money transfer for the attack, had been arrested. Two other men known as Khan and Riaz, but whose full names were not given, were also arrested. Two Pakistanis were arrested in Brescia, Italy (east of Milan) on 21 November 2009, after being accused of providing logistical support to the attacks and transferring more than US$200 to Internet accounts using a false ID. They had Red Corner Notices issued against them by Interpol for their suspected involvement and it was issued after the last year's strikes.

In October 2009, two Chicago men were arrested and charged by the FBI for involvement in "terrorism" abroad, David Coleman Headley and Tahawwur Hussain Rana. Headley, a Pakistani-American, was charged in November 2009 with scouting locations for the 2008 Mumbai attacks. Headley is reported to have posed as an American Jew and is believed to have links with militant Islamist groups based in Bangladesh. On 18 March 2010, Headley pleaded guilty to a dozen charges against him thereby avoiding going to trial.

In December 2009, the FBI charged Abdur Rehman Hashim Syed, a retired major in the Pakistani army, for planning the attacks in association with Headley.

On 15 January 2010, in a successful snatch operation R&AW agents nabbed Sheikh Abdul Khwaja, one of the handlers of the 26/11 attacks, chief of HuJI India operations and a most wanted suspect in India, from Colombo, Sri Lanka, and brought him over to Hyderabad, India for formal arrest.

On 25 June 2012, the Delhi Police Department arrested Zabiuddin Ansari alias Abu Hamza, one of the key suspects in the attack at the Indira Gandhi International Airport in New Delhi. His arrest was touted as the most significant development in the case since Kasab's arrest.Security agencies had been chasing him for three years in Delhi. Ansari is a Lashker-e-Taiba ultra and the Hindi tutor of the 10 attackers who were responsible for the Mumbai attacks in 2008. He was apprehended, after he was arrested and deported to India by Saudi Intelligence officials as per official request by Indian authorities. After Ansari's arrest, investigations revealed that in 2009 he allegedly stayed for a day in a room in Old Legislators's Hostel, belonging to Fauzia Khan, a former MLA and minister in Maharashtra Government. The minister, however, denied having any links with him. Home Minister P. Chidambaram asserted that Ansari was provided a safe place in Pakistan and was present in the control room, which could not have been established without active State support. Ansari's interrogation further revealed that Sajid Mir and a Pakistani Army major visited India under fake names as cricket spectators to survey targets in Delhi and Mumbai for about a fortnight.

A number of suspects were also arrested on false charges. At least two of them spent nearly eight years in prison and were not paid any compensation by the Indian government.

CHAPTER TWO

After of the 2008 Mumbai attacks

- After of the 2008 Mumbai attacks

The attacks are sometimes referred to in India as "26/11", after the date in 2008 that the attacks began. The Pradhan Inquiry Commission, appointed by the Maharashtra government, produced a report that was tabled before the legislative assembly more than a year after the events. The report said the "war-like" attack was beyond the capacity to respond of any police force, but also found fault with the Mumbai Police Commissioner Hasan Gafoor's lack of leadership during the crisis.

The Maharashtra government planned to buy 36 speed boats to patrol the coastal areas and several helicopters for the same purpose. It also planned to create an anti-terror force called "Force One" and upgrade all the weapons that Mumbai police currently have. Prime Minister Manmohan Singh on an all-party conference declared that legal framework would be strengthened in the battle against "terrorism" and a federal anti-terrorist intelligence and investigation agency, like the FBI, will be set up soon to co-ordinate action against "terrorism".The government strengthened anti-terror laws with UAPA 2008, and the federal National Investigation Agency was formed.

The attacks further strained India's slowly recovering relationship with Pakistan. India's then External Affairs Minister Pranab Mukherjee declared that India may indulge in military strikes against terror camps in Pakistan to protect its territorial integrity. There were also after-effects on the United States's relationships with both countries, the US-led NATO war in Afghanistan, and on the Global War on Terror. FBI chief Robert Mueller praised the "unprecedented cooperation" between American and Indian intelligence agencies over the Mumbai terror attack probe. However, Interpol secretary general Ronald Noble said that Indian intelligence agencies did not share any information with Interpol.

A new National Counter Terrorism Centre (NCTC) was proposed to be set up by the then-Home Minister P. Chidambaram as an office to collect, collate, summarise, integrate, analyse, co-ordinate and report all information and inputs received from various intelligence agencies, state police departments, and other ministries and their departments.

- Movement of troops

Pakistan moved troops towards the border with India voicing concerns about the Indian government's possible plans to launch attacks on Pakistani soil if it did not co-operate. After days of talks, the Pakistan government, however, decided to start moving troops away from the border.

- Reactions to the 2008 Mumbai attacks

Candlelight vigils at the Gateway of India in Mumbai

Indians criticised their political leaders after the attacks, saying that their ineptness was partly responsible. The Times of India commented on its front page that "Our politicians fiddle as innocents die."Political reactions in Mumbai and India included a range of resignations and political changes, including the resignations of Minister for Home Affairs Shivraj Patil, Chief Minister Vilasrao Deshmukh and deputy chief minister R. R. Patil for controversial reactions to the attack including taking the former's son and Bollywood director Ram Gopal Verma to tour the damaged Taj Hotel and the latters remarks that the attacks were not a big deal in such a large city.

- Indian Muslims condemned the attacks and refused to bury the attackers. Groups of Muslims marched against the attacks and mosques observed silence. Prominent Muslim personalities such as Bollywood actor Aamir Khan appealed to their community members in the country to observe Eid al-Adha as a day of mourning on 9 December. The business establishment also reacted, with changes to transport, and requests for an increase in self-defence capabilities. The attacks also triggered a chain of citizens‘ movements across India such as the India

Today Group's "War Against Terror" campaign. There were vigils held across all of India with candles and placards commemorating the victims of the attacks.The NSG commandos based in Delhi also met criticism for taking ten hours to reach the three sites under attack.Citizens gather outside The Taj Mahal Palace Hotel demanding the government take action.

International reaction for the attacks was widespread, with many countries and international organisations condemning the attacks and expressing their condolences to the civilian victims. Many important personalities around the world also condemned the attacks.

Media coverage highlighted the use of social media and social networking tools, including Twitter and Flickr, in spreading information about the attacks. In addition, many Indian bloggers offered live textual coverage of the attacks. A map of the attacks was set up by a web journalist using Google Maps.The New York Times, in July 2009, described the event as "what may be the most well-documented terrorist attack anywhere".

In November 2010, families of American victims of the attacks filed a lawsuit in Brooklyn, New York, naming Lt. Gen. Ahmed Shuja Pasha, chief of the ISI, as being complicit in the Mumbai attacks. On 22 September 2011, the attack on the American Embassy in Afghanistan was attributed to Pakistan via cell phone records identical to the attacks in Mumbai, also linked to Pakistan.

- Kasab's trial

Kasab's trial was delayed due to legal issues, as many Indian lawyers were unwilling to represent him. A Mumbai Bar Association passed a resolution proclaiming that none of its members would represent Kasab. However, the Chief Justice of India stated that Kasab needed a lawyer for a fair trial. A lawyer for Kasab was eventually found, but was replaced due to a conflict of interest. On 25 February 2009, Indian investigators filed an 11,000-page chargesheet, formally charging Kasab with murder, conspiracy, and waging war against India among other charges.

Kasab's trial began on 23 March 2009, and he pled not guilty on 6 May 2009. On 10 June 2009, Devika Rotawan, a child who had been shot in her leg during the attack, identified Kasab as one of the attackers during her testimony. He pled guilty on 20 July 2009. The judge found many of the

86 charges were not addressed in his confession, and therefore the trial continued 23 July 2009. Kasab initially apologised for the attacks and said he deserved the death penalty for his crimes, but on 18 December 2009, retracted his confession, and said he had been forced by police to make his confession.

Kasab was convicted of all 86 charges on 3 May 2010. He was found guilty of murder for directly killing seven people, conspiracy to commit murder for the deaths of the 164 people killed in the three-day terror siege, waging war against India, causing terror, and of conspiracy to murder two high-ranking police officers. On 6 May 2010, he was sentenced to death by hanging.[However, he appealed his sentence at high court. On 21 February 2011, the Bombay High Court upheld the death sentence of Kasab, dismissing his appeal.

On 29 August 2012, the Indian Supreme Court upheld the death sentence for Kasab. The court stated, "We are left with no option but to award death penalty. The primary and foremost offence committed by Kasab is waging war against the Government of India". The verdict followed 10 weeks of appeal hearings, and was decided by a two-judge Supreme Court panel, which was led by Judge Aftab Alam. The panel rejected arguments that Kasab was denied a free and fair trial.

Kasab filed a mercy petition with the President of India, which was rejected on 5 November. Kasab was hanged in Pune's Yerwada jail in secret on 21 November 2012 at 7:30 AM named as operation 'X'. The Indian mission in Islamabad informed the Pakistan government about Kasab's hanging through a letter. Pakistan refused to take the letter, which was then faxed to them. His family in Pakistan was sent news of his hanging via a courier.

- In Pakistan

Indian and Pakistani police exchanged DNA evidence, photographs and items found with the attackers to piece together a detailed portrait of the Mumbai plot. Police in Pakistan arrested seven people, including Hammad Amin Sadiq, a homoeopathic pharmacist, who arranged bank accounts and secured supplies. Sadiq and six others began their formal trial on 3 October 2009 in Pakistan. Indian authorities said the prosecution stopped well short of top Lashkar leaders. In November 2009, Indian Prime Minister Manmohan Singh said that Pakistan had not done enough to bring the perpetrators of the attacks to justice.

An eight-member commission comprising defence lawyers, prosecutors and a court official was allowed to travel to India on 15 March 2013 to gather evidence for the prosecution of seven suspects linked to the 2008 Mumbai attacks. However, the defence lawyers were barred from cross-examining the four prosecution witnesses in the case including Ajmal Kasab. On the eve of the first anniversary of 26/11, a Pakistani anti-terror court formally charged seven accused, including LeT operations commander Zaki ur Rehman Lakhvi. However, the actual trial started on 5 May 2012. The Pakistani court conducting trial of Mumbai attacks accused, reserved its judgement on the application filed by Lakhvi, challenging the report of the judicial panel, to 17 July 2012.

On 17 July 2012, the court refused to take the findings of the Pakistani judicial commission as part of the evidence. However, it ruled that if a new agreement, which allows the panel's examination of witnesses, is reached, the prosecution may make an application for sending the panel to Mumbai. The Indian Government, upset over the court ruling, however, contended that evidence collected by the Pakistani judicial panel has evidential value to punish all those involved in the attack. On 21 September 2013, a Pakistani judicial commission arrived in India to carry out the investigation and to cross examine the witnesses. This is the second such visit: the one in March 2012 was not a success as its report was rejected by an anti-terrorism court in Pakistan due to lack of evidence.

- In the United States

The LeT operative David Headley (born Daood Sayed Gilani) in his testimony before a Chicago federal court during co-accused Tahawwur Rana's trial revealed that Mumbai Chabad House was added to the list of targets for surveillance given by his Inter Services Intelligence handler Major Iqbal, though the Oberoi Hotel, one of the sites attacked, was not originally on the list. On 10 June 2011, Tahawwur Rana was acquitted of plotting the 2008 Mumbai attacks, but was held guilty on two other charges.He was sentenced to 14 years in federal prison on 17 January 2013.

David Headley pleaded guilty to 12 counts related to the attacks, including conspiracy to commit murder in India and aiding and abetting in the murder of six Americans. On 23 January 2013, he was sentenced to 35 years in federal prison. His plea that he not be extradited to India, Pakistan or Denmark was accepted.

- Memorials

On the first anniversary of the event, the state paid homage to the victims of the attack. Force One—a new security force created by the Maharashtra government—staged a parade from Nariman Point to Chowpatty. Other memorials and candlelight vigils were also organised at the various locations where the attacks occurred.

Mumbai 26/11 Attacks memorial bearing the names of people killed at Chhatrapati Shivaji Terminus.On the second anniversary of the event, homage was again paid to the victims.On the 10th anniversary of the 26/11 Mumbai terror attacks, Nariman House, one of the several establishments that were targeted by the Lashkar-e-Taiba terrorists, were to be declared a memorial and renamed as Nariman Light House.

The Indian Express group hosts an annual memorial event, 26/11 - Stories of Strength, in Mumbai to pay homage to those killed in the ghastly terror attacks in the city in 2008. The memorial event started in 2016, is now organised at the Gateway of India and brings forth the inspiring stories of courage and strength of more than 100 survivors that the Indian Express has interviewed over the past decade. Actor Amitabh Bachchan has been the brand ambassador for the event over the years.

- Films

1. Hotel Mumbai (2019) is an American-Australian action thriller film directed by Anthony Maras and written by John Collee and Maras. It has come under criticism for omitting any reference to the role of Pakistan in the terror strikes.
2. The Attacks of 26/11 (2013) is an Indian action thriller film directed by Ram Gopal Varma, depicting the attacks.
3. Taj Mahal (2015) is a French-Belgian thriller-drama film directed and written by Nicolas Saada. It was screened in the Horizons section at the 72nd Venice International Film Festival. The film is about an 18-year-old French girl who was alone in her hotel room when the terrorists attacked the hotel.
4. Terror in Mumbai (2009) features audio tapes of the intercepted phone calls between the young gunmen and their controllers in Pakistan, and

testimony from the sole surviving gunman.

5. Mumbai Siege: 4 Days of Terror (also known as One Less God) (2017) features the situation of some foreigners inside Taj Hotel.
6. State of Siege: 26/11 (2020) is an Indian Hindi-language web series released on ZEE5, showing the attacks from the perspective of NSG Commandos.
7. Mumbai Diaries 26/11 (2021) is an Indian Hindi-language medical drama series on Amazon Prime Video. The series is directed by Nikhil Advani and Nikhil Gonsalves. It follows the staff of Bombay General Hospital during the night of the attacks.

CHAPTER THREE

1993 Bombay bombings

- 1993 Bombay bombings

The 1993 Bombay bombings were a series of 12 terrorist bombings that took place in Mumbai, then known as Bombay, India, on 12 March 1993. The single-day attacks resulted in 257 fatalities and 1,400 injuries.

The attacks were reported to be coordinated by Dawood Ibrahim, leader of the Mumbai-based international organised crime syndicate D-Company. Ibrahim was believed to have ordered and helped organize the bombings through his subordinates Tiger Memon and Yakub Memon.

The Supreme Court of India gave its judgement on 21 March 2013, after over 20 years of judicial proceedings, upholding the death sentence against suspected ringleader Yakub Memon while commuting the previous death sentences against 10 others to life in prison.However, two of the main suspects in the case, Dawood Ibrahim and Tiger Memon, have not yet been arrested or tried. After India's three-judge Supreme Court bench rejected his curative petition, saying the grounds raised by him do not fall within the principles laid down by the apex court in 2002,the Maharashtra state government executed Yakub Memon on 30 July 2015.

In December 1992 and January 1993, there was widespread rioting throughout the nation following the Babri Masjid demolition in Ayodhya, where some of the most notable riots occurred in Bombay. Five years after the December–January riots, the Srikrishna Commission report found that 900 individuals had died and over 2,000 had been injured.

- Confession of Gul Mohammed

On 9 March 1993, three days before the bombings took place, a small-time criminal from the Behrampada slum in Northeast Mumbai named Gul Noor Mohammad Sheikh (Gullu) was detained at the Nag Pada police station. A participant in the communal riots that had rocked Mumbai the previous year, Gullu was also one of the 19 men handpicked by Tiger Memon, whose office was burnt in the riots. Tiger was a silver smuggler and chief mastermind of the bombings, for training in the use of guns and bomb making.

Gullu had been sent to Pakistan via Dubai on 19 February 1993 and upon completion of his training returned to Mumbai on 4 March. In his absence the police had detained Gullu's brothers to encourage him to surrender, which he did. He confessed to his role in the riots, his training in Pakistan, and a conspiracy underway to bomb major locations around the city, including the Bombay Stock Exchange, Sahar International Airport and the Sena Bhavan. However, his conspiracy claim was dismissed by the police as "mere bluff".

The arrest of Gul Mohammed spurred Tiger Memon to advance the date of the bombings which had originally been planned to coincide with the Shiv Jayanti celebrations in April 1993.

- The bombings

At 13:30 hours on 12 March 1993, a powerful car bomb exploded in the basement of the Bombay Stock Exchange building. The 28-story office building was severely damaged and many nearby office buildings also suffered damage. Reports indicate that 50 were killed by this explosion.About 30 minutes later, another car bomb exploded in front of the Mandvi branch of Corporation Bank near Masjid. From 13:30 hours to 15:40 hours a total of 12 bombs exploded throughout Mumbai. Most of the bombs were car bombs but some were in scooters.

Three hotels – the Hotel Sea Rock, Hotel Juhu Centaur, and Hotel Airport Centaur – were targeted by suitcase bombs left in rooms booked by the perpetrators.Banks, the regional passport office, the Air India Building, and a major shopping complex were also hit. Bombs exploded at Zaveri Bazaar and opposite it a jeep-bomb exploded at the Century Bazaar.Grenades were thrown at Sahar International Airport and at Fishermen's Colony, apparently targeting certain citizens at the latter. A double-decker bus was very badly damaged in the deadliest explosion, with as many as 90 people killed.

- After

The official number of fatalities was 257 with 1,400 others injured (some sources reported that 317 people died this misreport was due to a bomb which killed 69 in Calcutta on 16 March and was not part of 12 March Bombay bombings).

On 10 July 2006, the Chief Minister of Maharashtra, Sharad Pawar, admitted that he had "deliberately misled" people following the 1993 Mumbai bombings by saying there were "13 and not 12" explosions and had added the name of a Muslim-dominated locality to show that people from both communities had been affected.He attempted to justify this deception by claiming that it was a move to prevent communal riots by falsely portraying that both Hindu and Muslim communities in the city had been affected adversely. He also admitted to lying about evidence recovered and misleading people into believing that it pointed to the Tamil Tigers as possible suspects.

The bombings also caused a major rift within D-Company, the most powerful criminal organisation in the Mumbai underworld, headed by Dawood Ibrahim. Infuriated at the bombings, Ibrahim's right-hand man, Chotta Rajan, split from the organisation and took most of the leadership-level Hindu aides with him, including Sadhu, Jaspal Singh and Mohan Kotiyan. Rajan's split divided the Mumbai underworld along communal lines and pitted Chhota Rajan's predominantly Hindu gang against Dawood Ibrahim's predominantly Muslim D-Company. The ensuing gang war took the lives of more than a hundred gangsters and continues in 2017. Seven of the accused (Salim Kurla, Majeed Khan, Shakil Ahmed, Mohammed Jindran, Hanif Kadawala, Akbar Abu Sama Khan and Mohammed Latif) were assassinated by Rajan's hitmen.

- Arrests, convictions and verdict

Many hundreds of people were arrested and detained in the Indian courts. In 2006, 100 of 129 accused were found to be guilty and were convicted by Justice PD Kode of the specially designated Terrorist and Disruptive Activities (Prevention) Act (TADA) court. Many of those convicted have eluded custody, including the mastermind of the attacks,

Tiger Memon.

On 12 September 2006, the special TADA court convicted four members of the Memon family[38] on charges of conspiring and abetting acts of terror. They face jail terms from five years to life imprisonment, that would be determined based on the severity of their crime. Three other members of the Memon family were acquitted with the judge giving them the benefit of the doubt.

Yakub Memon was charged for possession of unauthorised arms. After the bombings, family members of Tiger Memon, including Yakub, escaped to Dubai and Pakistan. Correspondents say Tiger owned a restaurant in Mumbai and was allegedly closely associated with Dawood Ibrahim, the suspected mastermind.

Except for Tiger and Yakub, the entire family returned to India and were promptly arrested by the Central Bureau of Investigation in 1994. Yakub was later taken into custody and was undergoing treatment for depression. The Memon family was tried in court and found guilty of conspiracy. The defence lawyers asked for leniency in the sentencing and caused delays in the process.

- Yakub Memon was executed by hanging in Nagpur Central Jail at 6:35 a.m. IST on 30 July 2015

Two of the accused, Mohammed Umar Khatlab and Badshah Khan (pseudonym given by the prosecution to hide his real identity) turned state approvers.

Dawood Ibrahim, believed to have masterminded the terrorist attacks, is the Don of the Mumbai organised crime syndicate D-Company. He is suspected of having connections to terrorist elements such as al-Qaeda and its leader, Osama bin Laden, as well as Lashkar-e-Toiba, and was declared a terrorist by the governments of India and the United States in 2003. Ibrahim is now wanted by Interpol as a part of the worldwide terror syndicate of Osama bin Laden. He has been in hiding since the bombings and is living in white house, karachi, Pakistan, which the Pakistani government denied previously but accepted on 22 August 2020. The Bush administration in the United States imposed sanctions on Ibrahim in 2006.

The penalty stage of the longest-running trial in India's history continued. In February 2007, prosecutors asked for the death penalty for 44 of the 100 convicted. The prosecution also requested the death penalty for those convicted of conspiracy in the case. Asghar Yusuf Mukadam and Shahnawaz Qureshi, who have been found guilty for involvement in the bombings pleaded for leniency, claiming that they were not terrorists and were emotionally driven to participate in the act. Mukadam claimed that the main conspirators took advantage of his "frame of mind" after the demolition of Babri Masjid and the subsequent riots, alleging police partiality during the riots. "Vested interests" instigated him to act as he did. Quareshi was trained in Pakistan to handle arms and ammunition. He and Muquddam parked the explosive-filled vehicle at Plaza cinema which resulted in 10 deaths and 37 injuries. Qureshi reached Pakistan via Dubai, where he claims he was taken "under the pretext of providing ... an alternative job". He claims that his house was set on fire during the riots.

Some of the conspirators who managed to flee India after the bombings were arrested and extradited to India. These conspirators were declared absconders during the course of the trial. Abu Salem, Mustafa Dossa, Firoz Khan, Taher Merchant, Riyaz Siddiqui, Karimullah Khan, and Abdul Kayoum amongst others were arrested and the trial continued against these absconders in a special TADA court in Mumbai. Ujjwal Nikam who was earlier the Special Prosecutor in these case was replaced by Deepak Salvi to continue with the trial in the light of the subsequent developments. On 16 June 2017 gangster Mustafa Dossa and Firoz Khan were found guilty of conspiracy, which can carry the death penalty. On 26 June 2017 Dossa died of cardiac arrest in a Mumbai Hospital. Kayoom Sheikh was acquitted due to lack of evidence.

CHAPTER FOUR

Remembering the heroes of Mumbai attack

- 26/11 Mumbai Terror Attacks: Remembering the heroes of Mumbai attack

Amid the shock, rage, mourning, and terror that took over Mumbai, there were also incredible stories of courage from the Maximum City.

The 26/11 Mumbai terror attacks left a stain on the city's psyche, one of which has struggled to come to terms with. As many as 10 Pakistani terrorists from the sea targeted Chhatrapati Shivaji Terminus (CST) railway station, Nariman House Complex, Leopold Cafe, Taj Hotel and Tower, Oberoi-Trident Hotel, and Cama Hospital, among the prominent locations in South Mumbai. When the catastrophe ended after three days, 190 people were killed, and hundreds were injured.

1. 26/11 Mumbai Terror Attack was Pakistan sponsored

Grief, shock, anger, and horror came with the tragic incident in Mumbai 13 years ago, that came on November 26, 2008. While trying to save others, they faced the bullets of the terrorists, who fought back against terror. Some of these braves made the ultimate sacrifice. As we remember 26/11, let us also pause and remember some of these heroes.

2. Hemant Karkare, Ashok Kamte, Vijay Salaskar

Hemant Karkare, head of the Mumbai Anti-Terrorism Squad, was at his home in Dadar on 26 November at 9.45 PM to call about the terror attack. He immediately left for the CST station with his driver and bodyguard. There he came to know that the terrorists were now near Cama Hospital. Along with police officers Ashok Kamte and Vijay Salaskar, Karkare believed the two terrorists to be hiding behind a red car. Eventually, he saw one of the terrorists and managed to injure the only terrorist, Ajmal Kasab, who was caught alive. Still, in exchange for fire with another terrorist in a narrow lane close to the crime branch office, all three police officers were killed.

3. Tukaram Omble

The Mumbai Police, an army ex-soldier, Tukaram Omblay, and his fellow policemen were involved in a shootout in the hijacked car along with two terrorists, one of whom was killed. In the act of incredible courage, Omble grabs the barrel of Kasab's gun and takes dozens of bullets at point-blank range. Gave time to other police to defeat Kasab. For his supreme sacrifice, Omble was awarded the Ashoka Chakra, the country's highest peacetime gallantry award.

4. Major Sandeep Unnikrishnan

A member of the elite Special Forces, Major Sandeep Unnikrishnan, made the supreme sacrifice, defending fellow NSG commandos of 51 Special Action Groups and guests and combating terrorists inside the Taj Hotel. He was killed while fighting a terrorist armed with grenades and an AK-47 after being charged alone in a corridor. The 'Black Cat' managed to arrest a terrorist and take all the jihadists down to the restaurant, from which no one escaped the security forces' closure. Major Unnikrishnan was posthumously awarded the Ashoka Chakra.

5. Karambir Singh Kang

Not all heroes wear uniforms. Karambir Singh Kang was the Taj Mahal Palace Hotel's general manager in 2008 when the terrorist attack took place. He helped hundreds of guests and staff escape when the world around them fell drastically, keeping them calm. Although Kang himself survived the attack, his wife and two children did not make it and were killed in a fire going through the sixth floor.

CHAPTER FIVE

Thirteen years of seeking justice for the victims of 26/ 11 Mumbai terror attacks

- Thirteen years of seeking justice for the victims of 26/11 Mumbai terror attacks

November 26, 2021

On the 13th anniversary of the 26/11 Mumbai terrorist attacks, the Government and people of India somberly remember the victims of this dastardly attack and the valiant security personnel who laid down their lives to protect ours.

The President, Prime Minister and External Affairs Minister, in separate messages, have expressed their firm solidarity with the families of the victims.

A solemn memorial event was organised earlier today by the State Government of Maharashtra at the Police Memorial in Mumbai.

A senior diplomat from the High Commission of Pakistan in India was summoned by the Ministry of External Affairs today. A Note Verbale reiterating India's call for an expeditious trial in the Mumbai terror attacks case, and calling on the Government of Pakistan to abide by its commitment to not allow territories under its control for terrorism against India, was handed over to him.

Fourteen other countries lost their nationals in these attacks. Indian Missions in these countries are organizing memorial events remembering the victims, both national and foreign, reminding the world of the continuing global threat of terrorism. Senior government representatives from the host Governments, family members of victims and survivors will be participating in these solemn events.

It is a matter of deep anguish that even after 13 years of this heinous terror attack, the families of 166 victims from 15 countries across the globe still await closure, with Pakistan showing little sincerity in bringing the perpetrators to justice.

The 26/11 terrorist attack was planned, executed and launched from Pakistani territory. The former Prime Minister of Pakistan had gone on record and admitted that the terrorists were sent from Pakistan's soil. We once again call on the Government of Pakistan to give up double standards and to expeditiously bring the perpetrators of the horrific attack to justice. This is not just a matter of Pakistan's accountability to the families of the innocent victims who fell to terrorists, but also an international obligation.

The Government of India will continue to make every effort to seek justice for the families of the victims and the martyrs.

New Delhi
November 26, 2021

9 798885 465274

Printed by Libri Plureos GmbH in Hamburg,
Germany